# Growing Pains

**Sara Arneberg**
# Growing Pains

First Edition 2024

Growing Pains

Illustrations: Sara Arneberg © 2024, All Rights Reserved.
Cover: Sara Arneberg © 2024, All Rights Reserved.
Publisher: BoD – Books on Demand, Stockholm, Sweden
Print: BoD – Books on Demand, Norderstedt, Germany
ISBN: 978-91-8057-665-9

*To the person holding this book;*
*I hope this is what you've been looking for*

# Poems in this collection

# Poems in this collection

# Introduction

Since my high school graduation in 2022 and the release of *a bouquet of poems,* life has changed quite drastically. I've gone through a breakup, I've lost a few friends, and I've struggled quite a lot with loneliness. That's why I'm so grateful to have had this project and to be able to let all my feelings and thoughts out by writing. It's like therapy for me.

In some ways this is the follow up of *a bouquet of poems*, but in others it's a whole different book. *Growing Pains* is more focused on life after high school, and the beginning of adulthood. It's about healing from the darkness in life and beginning to see the light, growing through the pain, and to notice the small things that make everything worth it. The poems are still written mostly about my life, about the struggles I've faced and needed to let go of. It's been difficult readjusting to this new stage in life, sometimes I feel like I'm barely holding on, and others I feel like I'm on top of the world. Either way the poems make it easier to grasp my emotions and come to terms with them.

Sometimes I wish I could go back to my teenage years, somehow they seemed easier, like a driving lesson before the real exam. But mostly I don't. They are a finished chapter of my life, just as *a bouquet of poems* is a finished book. Now I'm writing *Growing Pains* and living the new chapters of my life. I'm experiencing new things, meeting new people and getting to know who I really am when I'm not in school and surrounded by people I know.

I hope that you, the reader, who has picked up this book, will find some resemblance to your own life in these poems. That you will feel seen or less alone, knowing that I've too been through difficult times. I wish that you who are searching for inspiration will find it here, between the lines of my poetry. And lastly, I hope that you who are looking for another point of view will finally understand the other perspective. If you've picked this book up and thought that it might not be for you, think again. I'm sure there's a poem here for you, or for someone else in your life. Please, enjoy!

Sara Arneberg
@abouquetofpoems

*Sprout*

### *Crumbs of love*

The crumbs of love you were feeding me
I was too obsessed and couldn't see
I kept on begging you for more,
with hands together, knees on floor

Constantly seeking your validation
the absence, felt like rough starvation
I was like your bird of pleasure,
in my eyes you were gold like treasure

I chased anything you'd throw
like old bread tossed to one black crow
Though I should have known that love
isn't just crumbs fed to a dove

Love is affection, desire, devotion
not old crumbs of faint emotion
-s

### *The old you*

I tell you that I miss you,
even though you're here
but I really miss the old you,
who would hold me near

I miss the times I would see,
the love glimmer in your eyes
I really miss the days,
that you would not tell me the lies

With excitement in your walk,
and enthusiastic voice
you made me feel overjoyed,
that I was someone's choice

But now I tell you that I miss you,
though that's not really true
I really miss the old you,
'cause we both know that we're through
-s

### *When we're apart*

I love you, but soon you'll leave
Won't see you for a while, that's why I grieve

I miss you, although you're here
But soon you'll leave, that's what I fear

I want you, but soon you're gone
Though you're still here, everything is wrong

I feel broken, when we're apart
And soon you're gone, poor lonely heart
-s

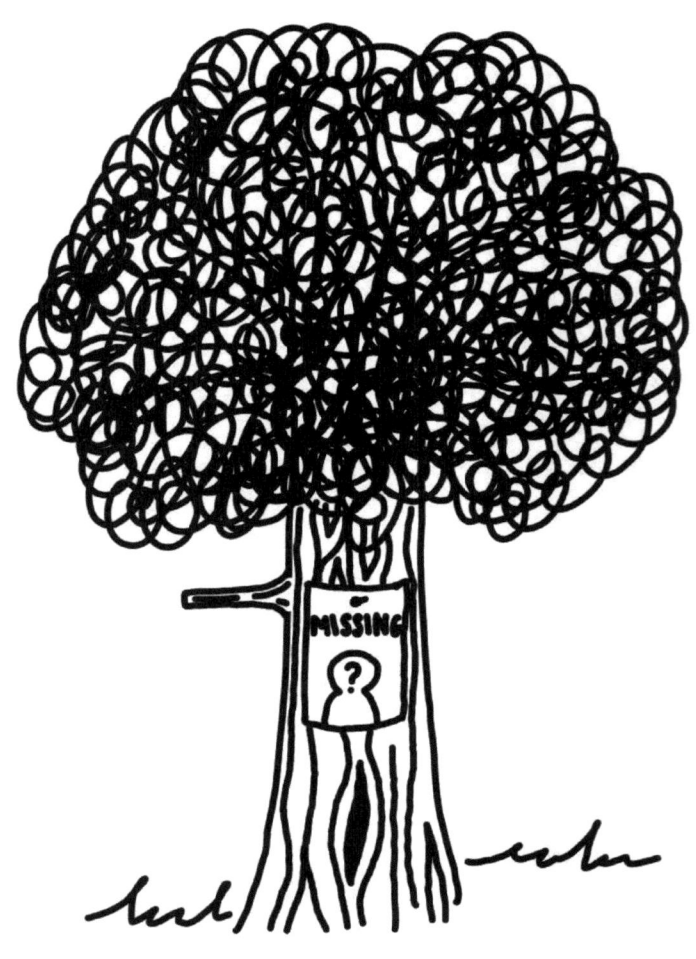

### *Missing person*
I still love you, I really do
I still wanna hug, and kiss you too

The sad thing is though; you don't feel the same
your voice is no longer soft, when you call my name

I miss all those fun and nice times we had
miss all those times where life felt so glad

How can you ever leave my heart?
you will always keep the biggest part
-s

### *My Heart*

My heart is torn,
when you break what you've sworn

My heart is broken,
when you don't keep what you've spoken

My heart is cracked,
when you don't speak the way you act

My heart is cold,
when you talk to me with that mouth of gold

My heart has died,
because of every single night I cried
-s

### *You're different now*

You're different now,
happier but totally different

I'm glad you found her, though
a part of me wishes you would remain the same

I wish you would have called, and asked me how I feel
I wish you would have called, and asked me how life is

You're different now,
happier but totally different

I'm glad you found her,
or at least that's what I try to tell myself
-s

### *All I wanted*

All I wanted was love,
being the one you put above

Your number one,
the sky to your sun

All I wanted was we,
so how couldn't I see

That we could never be
-s

### *Why is it always me?*

Why is it always me who apologizes first?
When it's always you who behaved the worst

Why is it always me who makes a call to you?
Even though you have nothing better to do

Why is it always me who cries late at night?
When you answer and say that you're alright

Why is it always me who initiates the kiss?
Even though you tell me I'm the one you've missed

Why is it always me who must fight?
When you are the one calling yourself my knight

Why is it always me who keeps us together?
Through sun, through rain, through stormy weather.
-s

### *Too much to ask*
Is it too much to ask, for a kiss on the cheek?
too much to ask for a date once a week?

Is it too much to ask, for a bouquet of flowers?
too much to ask for time that is only ours?

Is it too much to ask, for a handwritten letter?
too much to ask for us working to get better?

Is it too much to ask for, a hug around the hips?
too much to ask for a kiss on the lips?

Is it too much to ask for, all these small things?
maybe it's good we didn't buy the rings
-s

### *A sinking feeling*

In my chest, a sinking feeling
despite refusing, keep on kneeling

I chase every crumb you throw
no matter what, I am too slow

Your love, your affection
your hate, your rejection

Maybe it was best this way
that we together shouldn't stay

Putting myself first, I learn
before I any page can turn

In my chest, a sinking feeling
hoping it's because I'm healing
-s

### *Stolen*

My childhood years were stolen
and now my teenage years are too
I can't really grasp how I actually got through

The bullies in middle school
stabbed me deep and hard
For the rest of my life I will always be scarred

In high school things got better
made new friends and life was good
I thought this was my new life but of course it never would

Anxiety came crippling
depression came as well
I kept the whole thing quiet, felt like I could never tell

So, thank you to my bully
for ruining my person
with you my life has only gotten bad and then worsened

For you it was a small thing
something to do when you were bored
for me it is something that I'll always carry onboard
-s

### *Pearls of Fear*

The blade feels cold against my skin
goose bumps appear as soon as it touches
This is the closest, in a while I've been
to see the burgundy pierce the pale white

Break through to form dark pearls of fear
to uncover the thing that makes us alive
Just for it to sting and ache as it smears
The urge is so strong, I want to give in

I want to press the blade into the thin
want to press to break the fragile
to finally let go and let the urges win
but I can't get myself to destroy it

I can't let myself destroy the place
your gentle kisses against my wrist
can't imagine the look on your face
the next time you'd kiss me there
-s

### *The void in my chest*

There's a hole in my stomach,
there's a void in my chest
my heart is slowly dropping somewhere within my breast

There are stitches of sorrow,
there's darkness in my heart
I've been feeling this way every day since we part

There's pressure on my lungs,
there's sudden waves of crying
sometimes I think that I would rather just be dying

There are certain ways of coping,
there's mobile phone distractions
but most often I will turn to the riskier actions

There's hope in the hopeless,
there's sunshine after rain
but for some reason the only thing that saves me is the pain
-s

### *Retrospective*

In retrospect; when I look back
I finally manage to see the lack
of love, of need, of genuine care
of the interest to authentically share

I thought that you were telling the truth
but perhaps it was just my delusional youth
And the fact I did not want to believe
is now the sole reason for my grief

In retrospect; when I look back
I should've seen the enormous crack
But I convinced myself; it all was fine
and now the pain will be forever mine
-s

## *Cravings*

It hurts even more,
when you've lost what you had
when you've known life before,
everything got bad

Only a faint taste,
of the euphoric flavor left
of the people who were visitors
in the hotel of my chest

Memories to haunt me,
of what could have been
a desire of company,
at whom I could lean

A safe shell around my heart,
built out of trust
an exchange between two people,
that won't ever rust

I crave a person of which,
I can feed all my love
who can keep up with me,
and the thoughts I'm made out of

I need the closeness,
of someone who cares
it'll be a gift in the future,
if anyone dares
-s

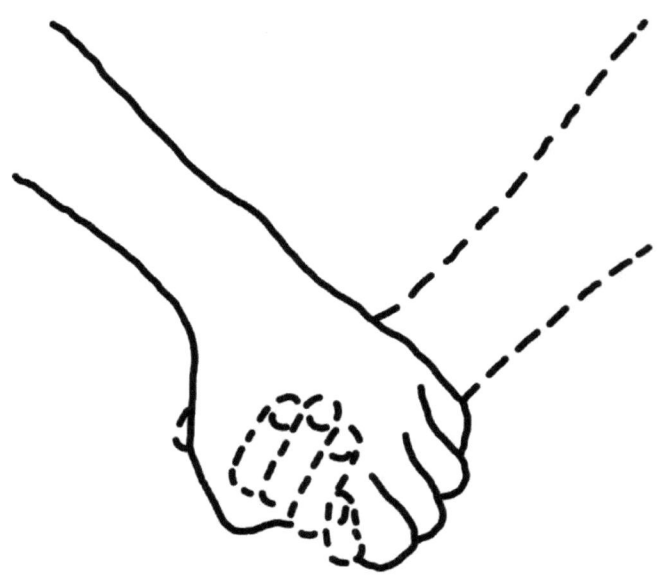

### *The everlasting cry*

Today I cried when I saw the sea
Remembering that's where you loved to be

I cried when I saw the flag of your land
I cry as I still feel the warmth of your hand

I cry as I passed a car just like yours
I cry as I wish I would have visited more

I cry when I remember the cake you use to make
I cry until all of my body starts to ache

I cry as I finally understand
That I never again will feel the warmth of your hand

I cry when I hear your name on the street
I cry until the ocean that you loved so much,
appears beneath  my feet
-s

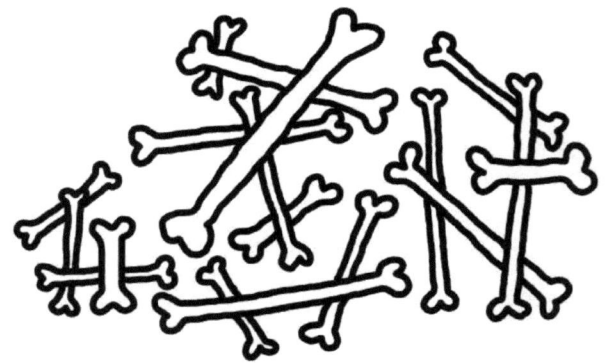

### *Realisation*

Something is different
I can feel the change
Your touch is colder
something is strange

Your stance is altered
I can feel the turn
deep in my bones
an excruciating burn

Your gaze is dull
the kisses quick
You've fallen out of love
I feel like I'm sick

When everything's over
my body is burned
Leave before it's late
or a lesson is learned
-s

### *Fade*

My arm has faded
so have my legs
there's only a faint shimmer
of where my body threads

It's eating me rapidly
like a fire without end
drowning me gently
until I no longer can fend

The emptiness haunts me
soon I'll be a ghost
as all my body fades
I'm closer to be whole
-s

## *Closing the Circle*

I have this fear that keeps me awake,
an underlying worry without any break

A thought that often crosses my mind
something that from birth to me was assigned

I'm afraid of death, I'm afraid of dying,
if I said something else I would have been lying

I'm afraid of dying, I'm afraid of death,
I'm afraid of the day I take my last breath

There's something so frightening about the unknown,
the thought of forever being all alone

It's something I think we inherent at birth,
the very same day we get put on this earth

The older one grows we get used to the fear,
when time has come and the end is near

I think death is something we welcome with ease,
to fully close the circle of life with some peace
-s

### *Autumn Blues*

I am terrified of autumn,
in case I fall back down
In case it will feel worse
as the leaves turn brown

Dark and gloomy mornings,
dark and gloomy nights
Afraid it will feel lonely
without the summer lights

Depressing gray season
strong wind, fog and rain
as the days grow short
I don't want to face the pain

I'm terrified of autumn
in case it turns out bad
In case it won't be different
and the dark still makes me sad
-s

*Growing*

### *I deserve better*

I deserve better,
when I'm always the one who writes
and the one to stay with you late nights

I deserve better,
when I'm the only one to call
and you don't even notice how I fall

I deserve better,
when the ideas are always mine
'cause you say they'll do just fine

I deserve better,
when you're so often on my mind
but still it's me that gets left behind

I deserve better,
when I try so hard to initiate
you'd think they wouldn't humiliate

I deserve better,
I'm doing my best to keep my friend
but it isn't working when only I am clicking send

I deserve better,
it's like talking to a wall;
I just fucking wish that you would call

I deserve better.
-s

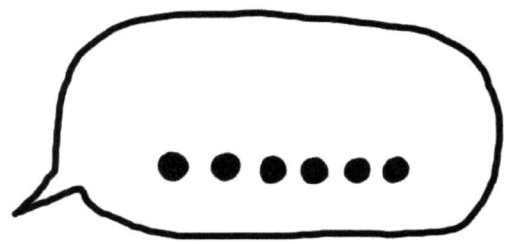

### *Empty words*
So empty are your words, because you really don't care
and it has always been this way, trust me I swear

You tell me you're so proud,
of all the things that I've done
In your eyes I search for stars,
though I know there are none

On social media you brag,
of what a good person I am
but in real life you never tell me,
that is such a scam

Your words are so empty,
because your actions show otherwise
I've known you for so long,
I've had time to realize

You promise things we will do,
but then you do them just alone
when I was younger I didn't get it,
but now I so much have grown

You tell me that you'll show up,
that you will wave to me and smile
then I cry after the play,
when I'd search for you a while

The most annoying thing is though, that I always still believe
but you let me down every time, I feel so fucking naïve
-s

## *Disappointment*

Of course there would be a last disappointment
a time where I once again would feel sad
Getting my hopes up for something fantastic
and ending up wishing that I should not have

You made me feel seen, like you really did care
with the promise that you told me you'd keep
how gullible of me to actually believe you
even when everything sounded so cheap

It's the last disappointment because from now on
I refuse to let him drag me down
The world will simply continue on spinning
let's just focus on turning my feelings around
-s

### *Erased*

I've come to realize, I'm no longer a priority
my title has downgraded from "best" to "friend"
I'm sure though, it's not your intent to offend
but it hurts me much to see this friendship end

I feel so alone, because you're still my number one
not a day goes by where I haven't thought of you
It's so incredibly obvious that I'm last in your queue
that you've replaced me with someone better and new

It seems to be so difficult to even get a text back
to be honest I'm disappointed, I thought I meant more
I had hoped I was enough to be part of your decor
Still I'm getting used to the darkness of your sock drawer

The history of us together is still present in my talk
it's easy to find you in my laugh, jokes and tone
I'm sure you've now got humor and puns of your own
I've been forgotten and erased from your known
-s

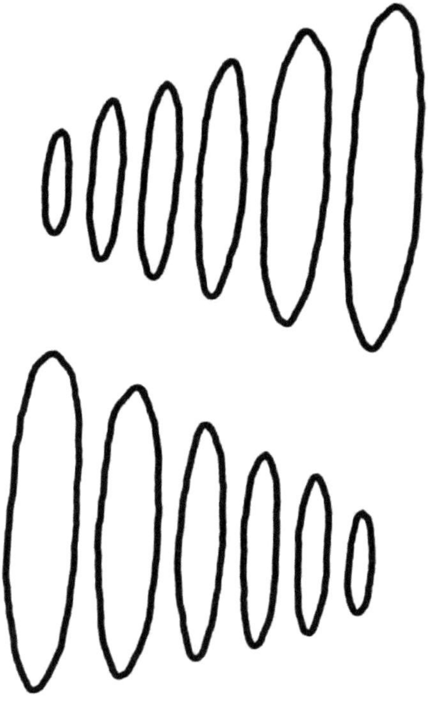

### *Regrets*

I was wrong, and didn't realize it for way too long
Now it's too late, you and I don't longer date

I shouldn't have treated you that way
There's an echo in my mind of what I said

It wasn't fair, I really regret it, I swear
I lay awake at night, wish to go back, and do it right

I'm so incredibly sorry, I didn't want to hurt
But still, I pushed you harsh into the dirt

I want to make it up to you, but how I've got no clue
Maybe it's best to just let it be, let you do you, and me do me
-s

### The taste of his own medicine

I wish he understood
how he made me feel
That this wound
will take a long time to heal

I wish that he saw me
how I lay here and cry
Soaking some napkins
with tears from my eyes

Only then can I know
if he regrets what he's done
if he steps up and says "I'm sorry"
Or if he cowardly hides and run

Only then can I know
if his care is genuine
if he feels any remorse
Or continue as it's always been

I want him to feel
exactly like I do
for him to understand
that for me this is nothing new

I want him to feel
exactly like he made me
consumed by the doubt
no way to break free

For once in my life
I want the control
For us to change places
For me to take his roll

I want him to understand
that he's done me wrong
I won't take this anymore
it's been going on too long
-s

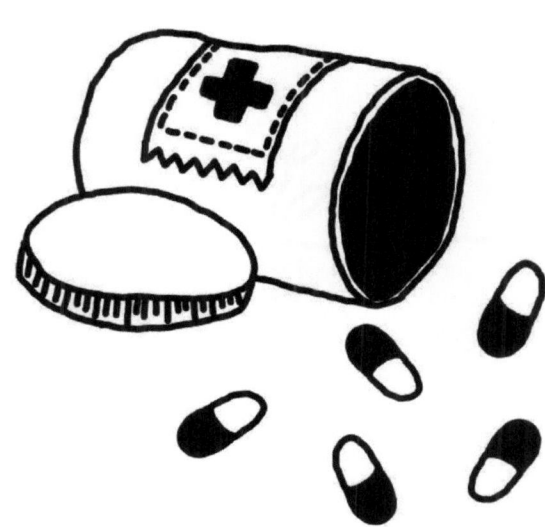

## *Too small to grow*

I don't like the word FOMO, fear of missing out
but it perfectly describes all of my self-doubt
The fear of still being, exactly the same
still sad and depressed, nothing new to my name

As they all move on, get a grip on what's ahead
I'm still living at home, fighting with the dead
I'm so incredibly jealous of all the nerve they've got
if I dared a little more, then maybe I too would have a shot

I want to do something drastic, just to prove that I can
prove that I'm no worse, that I too have got a plan
But anxiety holds me back, and will not let me go
it keeps me from flying, it keeps me too small to grow

Perhaps I should just do it, break free out of my shell
it could be the only thing, that breaks the cursing spell
I'll start with something small, something to get me going
then before I know it, I'll once again will be growing
-s

### *The Nice Girl*

I am the nice girl,
so sweet is my soul
to please everyone
that is my goal

I am the nice girl,
I'll be by your side
I say "it doesn't matter"
even though you made me cry

I am the nice girl,
always count on me
I'll cancel all my plans
to tell you that I'm free

I am the nice girl,
that all forget exists
taken for granted
still the sweetness persists
-s

### *The Forgiver*

"I'm sorry…"
*"It's fine"*
"You know, the fault wasn't mine"

"I'm sorry…"
*"It's okay"*
"I didn't mean it in that way"

"I'm sorry…"
*"Don't worry"*
"Everything is kind of blurry"

"I'm sorry…"
*"It's all right"*
"I did it out of fright"

*"I'm sorry"*
"Go away,
can't stand to see you another day"
-s

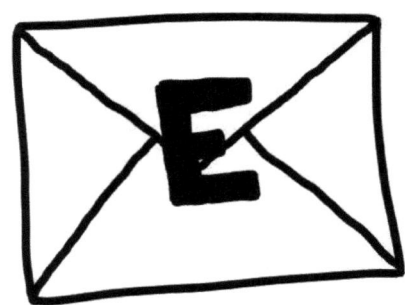

### *An Unsent Email*

There's an unsent email, meant for my boss
which has a very important point made across

About a co-worker, who's a little too close
who sends me pictures without his clothes

An email with beginning, a middle and an end
though still I can't seem to click and send

The what-ifs in my head, the worry in my brain
is it better to shut up and not complain?

There's an unsent email, I decided to delete
until another time when the story will repeat
-s

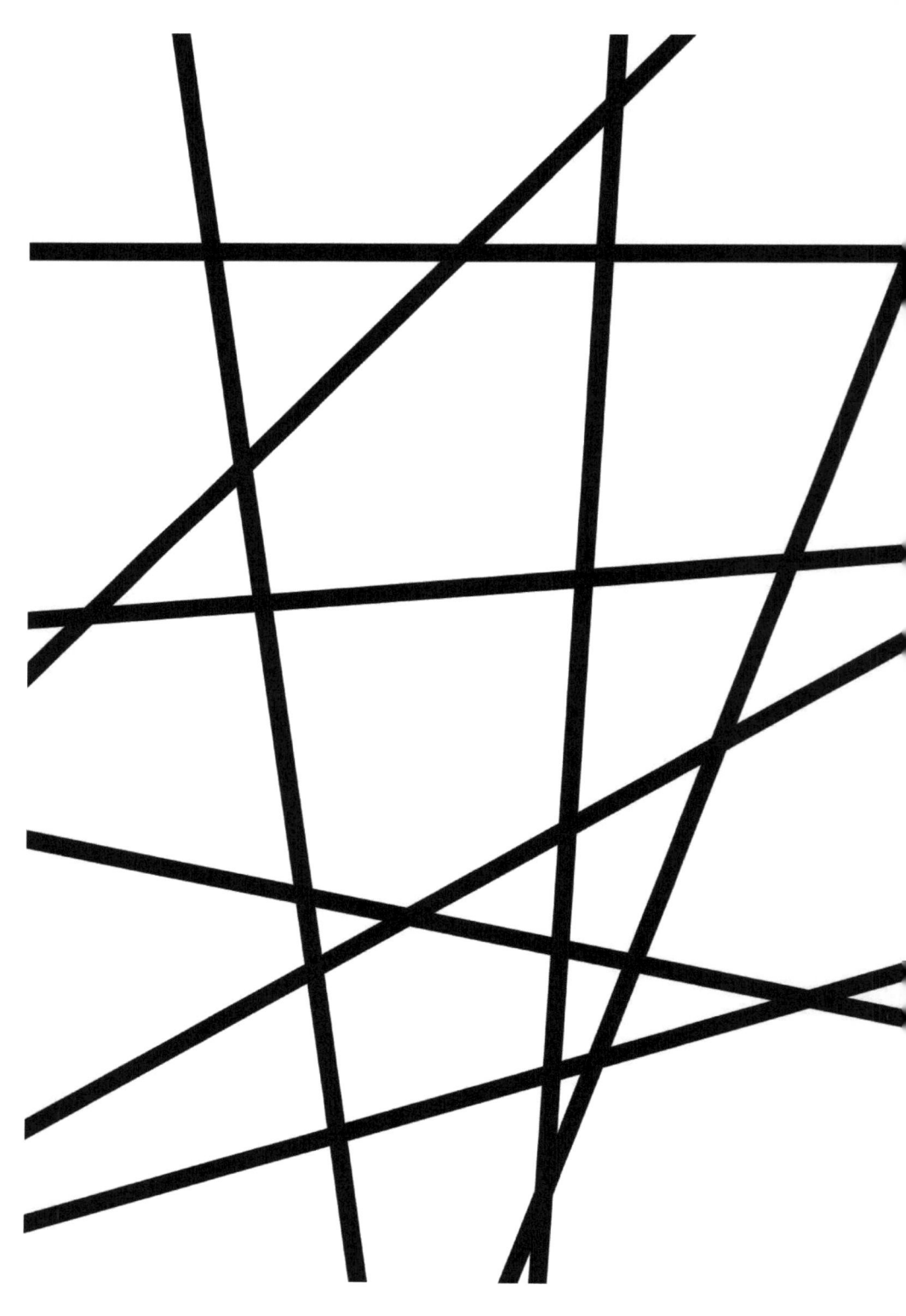

### *Against your lines*

I don't want to meet him,
why can't I say no?
I just want to hide,
why can't he just go?

Don't want to see him,
why do I keep saying yes?
Can't he just leave me alone?
This is way too much stress!

I don't want to kiss you boy,
what don't you understand?
I'm not your little toy,
this is getting out of hand!

My signals are so clear,
I am not sending out mixed signs
You just can't take a no,
when it's against your lines
-s

### The music shop

In the music shop on 2nd street
was the first time that we'd ever meet

We sang, we danced, we played all night
'till the sun came up and shined so bright

The songs we sang made time stand still
then you asked me if I ever will

Be just yours, yes only yours
I politely declined and you shut the doors

In the music shop on 2nd street
was the last time that we'd ever meet
-s

### *As night turns to dawn*

Fancy glass and cheap champagne
I watch as you try to explain

Legs crossed without high heels
dirty dishes from takeout meals

Radio with some faint jazz blues
on table flowers and yesterday's news

Candles that will soon burn down
noises from the world around

We are young, though the night ain't
in the distance; Apollo paints

A sunrise with orange and pink
You watch me pour another drink
-s

### *Fortune Cookie*

Happy news is on its way
expect the unexpected
Wait a while to take the step
or else you'll get rejected

Wealth awaits you very soon
if you take an opportunity
Love will then come back to you
when you help your community

Salt and sugar look the same
be careful who you trust
It might be difficult right now
but soon you will adjust
-s

## *Wonders of Summer*

The fragile leaves of poppies,
the weak petals of lily
The dark pink stalk of rhubarb,
the red hot fruit of chili

All wonders of nature,
in their own beautiful way
With colour, smell and taste,
to wish they'd forever stay

The tiny, juicy berries,
the sturdy large potatoes
The violet gradient of figs,
the shiny red tomatoes

All are happy memories,
of summer and of sun
But now it's fall and winter's
time to have a little fun
-s

### Trashcan roses

In the trashcan at the airport
lies a neat bouquet
of crimson coloured roses
made to give away

One can only imagine
who they were meant for
a last chance to get back
one who doesn't love anymore

Or maybe for someone
who'd already left
for a place far away to
finally get some rest

Perhaps they were
for one who didn't show
who promised to be there
with a sign on first row

In the trashcan at the airport
lies a neat bouquet
which didn't fulfill its purpose
it never got given away
-s

### *A new year's poem*
Happy New Year, my dear!
let's celebrate with laughs and cheer

It's the end of a tough time
let's together hear the bells chime

Watch all the pretty stars
Wish that the next year is ours

Kiss as the clock twelve turns
listen as the firework burns

Happy New Year, my dear!
in 365 days, I hope you're still here
-s

### *Lost time*

The emptiness is creeping,
as I realize the time
Coming closer to the day,
he did not want to be mine

Then kept the news away,
from me a whole half year
Acting just as normal,
could it be out of fear?

As I realize the time,
together long been lost
Time I won't get back,
time of priceless cost

I feel so empty deep inside,
a part of me is gone
Wishing he'd break up with me,
get it over with, be done

I'm taking back my time again,
these next months will be nice
Doing things because I want,
not thinking 'bout it twice
-s

### Female Rage

I fucking hate this
I hate them, I hate you
I hate everything
and now myself too

I wanna scream
I wanna fight
I wanna push
I wanna bite

I wanna stare at you
with such disgust
That your will to live
gets turned into dust

I fucking hate this
I hate them, I hate you
I hate everything
and now myself too
-s

## *Under the façade*

I thought you would be different
That you'd treat me as an equal
That you'd respect my boundaries
and listened to my needs

I thought you would be better
That you'd keep your promises
That you'd water my flowers
and not my murky weeds

And for a while you were
you were different, you were better
But things like that doesn't last
things like that won't be forever

Under the façade you were a copy
an exact replica, of all other men
Lying, shallow, irresponsible,
not capable of endeavor

I thought you would be different
and you were, but not enough
-s

*Bloom*

### *Your story*

Bruises like rainbows,
burgundy scratches
Old scars and
the burns from matches

Accidentally-made,
marks on our body
as a book the words
will reveal the story

Of a memory that,
won't ever disappear
because the reminder
on our body just here
-s

### *Strong by myself*

I wish you'd were there, when life felt so tough
I wish you'd were there when things were so rough

Keep telling myself it wouldn't have gone wrong
If you'd been there close by my side, all along

I needed you there, in my darkness alone
but you couldn't support, that's what you've shown

Still, in the end, everyone will die by themselves
perhaps, onwards; I should get strong by myself
-s

### *Opinion*

I'm tired of the comments
I know I am enough
My body isn't yours to think
even though you've had it rough

I'm tired of the comments
that are supposed to "help" me
You're not allowed an opinion
on the things that you can't see

I'm tired of the comments
"are you eating all of that?"
It's not even that much
Are you try'na call me fat?

I'm tired of the comments
"isn't that thing way too sweet?"
How about you care for yourself
and not what I choose to eat?

I'm tired of the comments
that you reflect from your inside
I know my worth, I know myself
I'm way too fed up to hide
-s

### *The Queen of Spades*

The Queen of Spades, an unlucky one
when turned upon, the game is done

She's got no one, to call her king
on her hand, there is no ring

But she knows better, she needs no man
she is perfectly capable of opening that can

The Queen of Spades, knows her worth
she knows her place on this earth

She knows herself, won't take no shit
The Queen of Spades will never quit
-s

### *The last letter*

In the last letter you wrote,
that you wouldn't, and I quote;
"ever want see my eyes",
they just "reminded you of lies"

The lies that your own heart created,
that you and I were in love and dated
But if you'd asked me I wouldn't say the same,
and for that you can't really give me the blame

You "don't want to hear my voice"
and if it were up to your choice
You wouldn't want to meet me for good,
HA! Why do you even reckon that *I* would?

But I know that you still think about me,
of that time with the picnic under the tree
Or the time that we took a coffee and talked,
and the time that we went for a stroll and just walked

No matter how much you want to forget,
we all know it will only make you regret
For I was "the best thing that's happened to you",
and now I'm the worst for putting you through

I know that you lay awake at night,
thinking 'bout the things you should've write
Though we all know this is my fight to win,
it was from the start and has always been
-s

### *How to be Woman 101*
Get used to feel unsafe at night,
walk only in the lamppost light

Get used to talk a whole lot less,
and guys who force you to say yes

Get used to being touched in ways,
and feel the burn of the male gaze

Get used to being mansplained to
of all the things you already knew

Get used to be the weaker sex,
only to be called his crazy ex

Get used to life not being fair,
and to constantly think about what you wear

If men were women for a day,
then maybe they would stop downplay

The problems and the trouble we face
on an ordinary day to day base
-s

### *How to be Man 101*

Get used to never show emotion,
and don't you dare to cry an ocean

Get used to being strong and stable
to work and bring food to the table

Get used to get denied on dates,
and then made fun of by your mates

Get used to feel so all alone,
when love for a while has not been shown

Get used to being scared to hurt,
when really, you're just trying to flirt

Get used to the pressure on your chest,
you need to be the family's best

If women were men for a day,
then maybe they would stop downplay

The problems and the trouble we face,
on an ordinary day to day base
-s

### *To the people I've cried leaving*

You are the ones I've cared about the most,
the ones that I'd much rather hold close
You are the people I've cried while leaving
the people who were always believing

To my high school French teacher,
to my year nine best friend
To my first ever boyfriend,
to my roommate from start to end

We both knew it was time to part,
that a new beginning just had to start
A time and age of things and change,
so sudden; everything felt strange

To my teacher in needlework,
to my jolly friend abroad
To my loving family and
my high school friend squad

You are the people I've cried while leaving,
the people who were always believing
You believed in me and my ridiculous being,
So thank you for sticking around and seeing
-s

### *The movie continues*
The movie continues,
with another script this time

Together you and I
up the mountain climb

Watch the lighthouse's
prism and lighting beams

Discover that everything
is not really what it seams

Practically alone
on this dark wide earth

You made me realize
my own great self-worth

The movie continues
with another script and plot

We'd leave the mountain stronger
or at least that's what I thought
-s

### *The first real love*
The first real love, will never leave my heart
always and forever of me he'll be a part

Memories of holding, his hand on the train
will sometimes reappear once again in my brain

Feelings that never, will leave me alone
remembering the smell of his favorite cologne

The first real love, will never leave my soul
but its things like that, that make a person whole
-s

### *It is temporary*

It's gonna be alright
feelings are temporary
Get used to the emotion
the duration may vary

If it feels like a spiral
like nothing makes sense
You're stuck inside your head
where everything's intense

It's gonna be alright
just take a big deep breath
However it feels
will not lead to your death

It's uncomfortable, I know
but it will not last for long
Just try to live your life
I know that you are strong
-s

### *I feel too much*

I feel too much
I feel so deep
One second I smile
the other I weep

I feel too much
I feel so strong
Life is wonderful
what can go wrong?

I feel too much
I feel so intense
everything sucks
nothing makes sense

I feel too much
but what can one do?
A flower can't bloom
without sun and rain too
-s

### *Someone*

Someone to touch, someone to hold
every day of our lives until we get old

A body to feel, a body to know
every month of the year as I watch you grow

When I found you, my beautiful boy
I laughed, and I laughed you bring me such joy

Then I cry, and I cry only happy tears
Oh my dear boy how you tackle my fears
-s

### *True or False*

Is this the way
loves supposed to be?

Is it you that
finally will set me free?

Is it you that
showed me love for real?

Is this the way
that I'll heal?

Yes, it is you,
all the answers are true
-s

### *The fascination of him*

I wanna bury my face in the depth of his neck
Reach up to his lips and give them a peck

I wanna touch and feel every corner of his soul
Gaze at his eyes that makes me feel so whole

I wanna kiss and embrace all his freckles and marks
Notice how he lays and how his back arcs

I wanna hug and cherish all his faults and his flaws
Observe how he smiles and how he clenches his jaws
-s

### *What if it's true?*

What if it's true?
All the things they say
What if it's true?
That I'm not so grey

Maybe they're right
I'm not as bad as I thought
Maybe they're right
I *am* worth a lot

Perhaps I should listen
I've got beautiful eyes
Perhaps I should listen
My heart is the biggest size

What if *I'm* wrong?
I *do* have a nice voice
What if *I'm* wrong?
To love myself *is* a choice
-s

### *Maple Syrup Voice*

I don't feel complete, without your hand in mine
tracing my fingers up and down your spine

Feeling your heart, beat fast just like a pattern
your brown eyes stunning, like the rings of Saturn

I don't feel at home, without your presence near
that maple syrup voice is all I want to hear

Chasing your hair strands, blowing in the breeze
your radiating warmth makes me feel at ease

I don't feel like myself, without you being around
all the scars on your body and the mole that I found

Your hair dark like feathers, of a majestic black raven
strong arms wrapped around me, like a safe old haven
-s

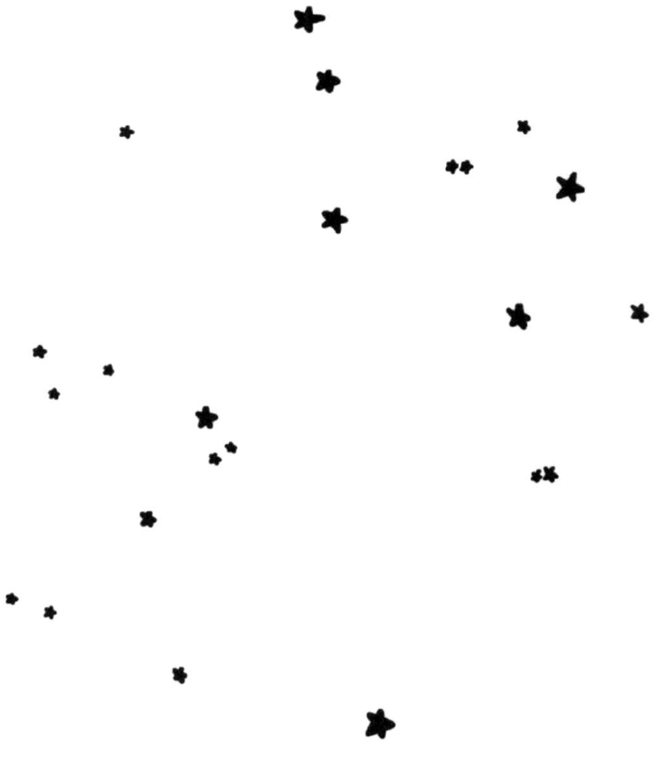

### *The life I live*

I love my smile, my cheeks
my heart that beats
I love my arms, my chest
and all the rest
The dark brown that surrounds my eye
my stomach, nose and even my thigh

I love my freckles, my spots
My stretch marks and dots
I love my legs, my arm hair
my skin that is fair
The wrinkle that on my forehead appears
my fingers, toes and ears that can hear

I love my teeth, my waist
my tongue with taste
I love my hips, my nails
and all other small details
But mostly I love how imperfect I am
how the only thing that matters is my poetry slam,

My creative mind,
the fact that I'm pretty much blind
And lastly, I love the kindness that I give
so, this is why; I love the life I live
-s

### *Magic in the Mundane*

There's magic in our nature
in the trees of the forest
in the waves of the sea
in the wind, blowing free

There's magic in the living
in the people of our hearts
in the animals of our land
in the ladybug on your hand

There's magic in the mundane
in the things we always see
in the mushroom on the path
on the bubbles in our bath

There's magic in our lives
if we just dare to notice
if we let go of our past
magic will find us, at last
-s

# Acknowledgements

Thank you to Oscar Strickland who's been a great editor, and hype man, along the way. I couldn't have wished for anyone more encouraging and supportive by my side.

A special thank you to the people in my life who've inspired some of these poems, you know who you are. Without *you* this book wouldn't exist, so thank you very much!

As in the last book, I want to thank myself. This has been, what has felt like, the loneliest year of my life. I feel so incredibly proud that I've managed to write this whole book even though I've still struggled a bit with my mental health and the readjustments into this new stage of life.

And at last, I once again want to thank you who are reading this book. It means the world to me that people are reading and appreciating my work and poetry. If you want to see more content and updates from my books, try to follow my social media @abouquetofpoems. Until next time!

*Sara Arneberg*

# About the author

Sara Arneberg is a twenty-year-old poet and writer born and raised in the south of Sweden. She began writing short stories as early as elementary school and continued throughout middle school. However, it was not until the later years of high school that she found a passion in writing poetry.

Struggling with her mental health was what began the poetry-writing for Sara. She turned to writing as a way to cope with the rough emotions and to let the feelings out instead of keeping them hidden inside. Even though she did not realise it back then, her poems would become popular amongst her friends and family.

In the fall of 2022 Sara debuted with her poetry collection, *a bouquet of poems*. A book containing a complete collection of poems written during her junior and senior years of high school. After a successful year, she's now releasing her second book, *Growing Pains*. With titles such as « Crumbs of Love », « I deserve better », and « Magic in the Mundane » this collection perfectly captures the journey of healing through rough times. Dealing with the pain, fighting the darkness and growing in the meantime.

# Read more by Sara Arneberg

Life is never what you expect it to be. Whatever you do to follow the plan, life always surprises you with the most amazing and horrible things. This collection of poems captures just that, all ups and downs of life. Both the good and the bad, the glad and the sad.

Though these poems mostly reflect a later teenage life, everyone can find some poems they resonate with. Whether it's the feminist frustration in « Woman's issue » or the timeless love of « Never thought I would have fell for you » there is something for everyone!

Browse through titles such as « Lighthouse Love », « Apple pie » and « There is this guy » while getting a peek into the author's colorful mind.

a bouquet of poems

Sara Arneberg